Anonymous

An Enquiry Into the Rights of the East-India Company of Making War and Peace

And of possessing their territorial acquisitions without the participation or

inspection of the British government: in a letter to the proprietors of

East-India stock

Anonymous

An Enquiry Into the Rights of the East-India Company of Making War and Peace
*And of possessing their territorial acquisitions without the participation or
inspection of the British government: in a letter to the proprietors of East-India
stock*

ISBN/EAN: 9783337012786

Printed in Europe, USA, Canada, Australia, Japan

Cover: Foto ©Suzi / pixelio.de

More available books at **www.hansebooks.com**

AN ENQUIRY INTO THE RIGHTS

OF THE

EAST-INDIA COMPANY

Of making WAR and PEACE;
and of poffeffing their
TERRITORIAL ACQUISITIONS
without the Participation or Infpection
of the BRITISH GOVERNMENT.

In a Letter
to the PROPRIETORS of EAST-INDIA STOCK.
Written in the Year 1769.
And now firft publifhed.

LONDON:
Printed for WALTER SHROPSHIRE in New
Bond-ftreet, and SAMUEL BLADON in
Pater-nofter Row.
M.DCC.LXXII.

PREFACE.

IT is long fince the nations, which have the misfortune to live near the Eaft-India Company's fettlements, have ftretched out their induftrious and helplefs hands to our gracious Sovereign, imploring his protection from the oppreffions they were finking under; and it muft give great pleafure to every one who knows how much the interefts of Great Britain are connected with thofe of humanity, to learn, from his Majefty's fpeech, at the opening of this feffion, that he had turned his eye to an object fo worthy of the royal attention. And, furely, if there is any fituation in this life more deplorable than another, it is that of living under the dominion of men, who, wholly intent upon gain, have contrived to eftablifh the moft complete fyftem ever known of fraud and violence.

violence, by uniting, in the fame perfons, the feveral functions of Merchant, Soldier, Financier and Judge; depriving, by that union, all thofe functions of their mutual checks, by which alone they can be made ufeful to fociety.

It is to be hoped that the time is not far off, when thofe functions, fo improperly combined, will be again feparated: when his Majefty will refume, from thofe Merchants, the fword, which, by our happy Conftitution, cannot be placed, with energy or fafety, in any hand but his own: and when thofe great territorial revenues in Bengal, which have, of late, been fo extravagantly accumulated in the coffers of private men, for trifling or deftructive purpofes, will be employed in reducing the national debt, as well as in protecting our trade and acquifitions in thofe diftant parts of the world. We might then hope to fee an impartial adminiftration of juftice in India, without its being fubject to the controul of thofe

who

who are moft likely to be the greateft delinquents. We might then hope to fee an end to thofe cruel monopolies, carried on by the Servants of the Company, in the neceffaries of life, and to which the wretched natives are obliged to fubmit, with the bayonet at their throats: and we might then hope to fee thofe Servants once more attentive to the commercial interefts of their employers; without attempting to equal, in riches and fplendor, the firft nobility of the kingdom. But, what is ftill of greater importance to the free Conftitution of this country, we might then hope to fee fome ftop put to the rapid progrefs of corruption at home; which has been, for fome years paft, fo much promoted by the immenfe fums lavifhed by thofe Servants of the Company, upon their return from India, in order to procure themfelves admittance into the Houfe of Commons; where none of them, from the nature of their education, can be fuppofed to have any thing

to

to say; and where some of them seem to come, as if they were proud of the privilege they had acquired, of mocking the insufficiency of our laws, and of insulting that honourable Assembly, by their presence.

In objection to this salutary change, it has been often urged, "That in a free "country like ours, the individuals have "their legal rights as well as the state; "and that it is always matter of just alarm "when the supreme legislative power lays "its heavy hand upon those rights, even "where there is reason to believe that "they have been abused." In this I entirely agree. But when they proceed to tell us, "That the East-India Company "have a legal right of making War and "Peace, and of possessing their territorial "acquisitions, without the participation "or inspection of the British Government," I find myself obliged to give my dissent. The grounds of that dissent are to be found in the following Letter, written above

above two years ago, when Sir JOHN LINDSAY was appointed to command his Majesty's ships in the East-Indies; and though the occasion which produces it now, is somewhat different from that which at first gave birth to it; yet I have suffered it to appear before the public in its original shape; and the rather, because in that shape it recalls the memory of a transaction, by which the true spirit of the Gentlemen who have the management of the Company's affairs in Leadenhall-street, had a fair opportunity of displaying itself.

London, Feb. 18, 1772.

A LETTER

A
LETTER

TO THE

PROPRIETORS OF EAST INDIA STOCK,

CONCERNING

The Company's Rights of making War
and Peace, &c.

GENTLEMEN,

I Was at your general meeting on Tuef-
day laft, and find, by a letter fent that
day by LORD WEYMOUTH, that the
difpute which has for fome time fubfifted
between the Miniftry and your Directors
is now fully explained, and reduced to this
fingle queftion, *Whether the officer appointed
to command his Majefty's fhips in the Eaft
Indies fhall be confulted, and have a voice, in
all matters relative to peace and war in thofe
parts?* To which I find the leading men

B   in

in the Direction are very defirous you fhould give a negative, faying, *that the King's Officer fhall be called in and confulted by the Supervifors, whenever they fhall ftand in need of his advice or affiftance, but that he fhould have no vote in the deliberation.*

Thefe are opinions very effentially different from one another; and which of the two will be moft conducive to the honour and intereft of the Company will fall upon you to determine at your next General Court, which is to be called for that purpofe. *

In the mean time, I could not help obferving the different tones with which thofe different pretenfions were urged on the fide of the Miniftry and on the fide of the Directors : for while his Majefty, through his Secretary of ftate, defired, in a moft gracious and condefcending manner, that

* It was then determined that the King's officer fhould not be admitted to any fhare with the fervants of the company, in their deliberations concerning peace or war.

that the Directors would *allow him some share of power* in the management of peace or war, the Directors, as if they had meant to exhibit to our view the Saturnalia of the ancient Romans, told us in an elevated ftrain, *that they had already, by their inftructions, given as much power to the King's officer as they thought convenient, and were not willing to give any more.*

Struck with the oddity of this fcene, I was once on my legs to afk from whence they derived thofe royal prerogatives of making peace and war, which they had, in fo unlimitted a manner, delegated to Meffrs VANSITTART, SCRAFTON, and FORDE, and of which they were fo unwilling to communicate a part to their Sovereign; but was faved that trouble by one of the twenty four, who told us, *that he would, to the utmoft of his power, fupport thefe rights of the Company, which were derived from acts of parliament, and royal Charters founded upon acts of parliament.*

Having got fo far into this enquiry, I refolved

I refolved to get to the bottom of it; and accordingly, upon my return home, gathered together all the Acts of parliament, and all the royal Charters, that had been made refpecting *this* Company, and will now communicate to you, my fellow Proprietors, what has occurred to me on the perufal of them; that fuch of you, as have not taken the fame pains, may be enabled to judge, whether the pretenfions to Sovereignty are beft founded at the eaft or at the weft end of the town.

The firft royal Charter given to *this* Company, and the firft that was ever founded on an Act of parliament, is that of the tenth year of King William III. in which all that is faid, with refpect to the powers of making peace or war, is comprifed in the following words: " *Such* " *governors or officers fhall and may, according* " *to the directions of the faid company, raife,* " *train and mufter fuch military forces as fhall* " *and may be neceffary for the defence of the* " *faid*

" *faid forts, places and plantations refpective-*
" *ly.*" Here is no power granted beyond
what every man feems to derive from the
Great Charter of God; to wit, that of de-
fending himfelf in the beft manner he can,
when that human power to which he owes
allegiance, and from which he has a right to
expect protection, is at too great a diftance
to afford it to him. Here is not the leaft
hint of this Sovereign power being
deprived of the right of interpofing its
advice and affiftance, whenever it fhall
think fuch advice or affiftance neceffary;
on the contrary, as if the prefent ridicu-
culous difpute had been forefeen, the
following words are added: " *The fovereign*
" *right, power and dominion over all the faid*
" *forts, places and plantations, to us, our*
" *heirs and fucceffors, being always referved.*"

In none of the fubfequent Charters is
there any thing worth obferving, with
regard to peace and war, 'till we come
to the Charter of the thirteenth of King
GEORGE I. and to that of the 26th of his
late

late Majefty, commonly called *the Charter of juftice*, where a variety of acts of hoftility are permitted to the Company, but ftill ftrictly confined in their caufe, as in the charter of King WILLIAM, to what is *defenfive* and what is *juft* only. The words are — " *To affemble, exercife in arms, martial,* " *array, and put in warlike pofture, the* " *inhabitants of the faid towns and places,* " *either by fea or land, for their efpecial* " *defence and fafety, and to lead and conduct* " *them, and to encounter, repulfe, expel and* " *refift, by force of arms, as well by fea, as* " *by land, and alfo to kill, flay and deftroy,* " *by all fitting ways, enterprizes and means* " *whatfoever, all and every fuch perfon or* " *perfons as fhall or may, at any time* " *hereafter, in a hoftile manner, attempt* " *or enterprize the deftruction, invafion,* " *detriment or annoyance of any of our fubjects* " *within the faid towns and factories and* " *limits, or any of their fervants, or perfons* " *dealing with them; and in time of war,* " *or open hoftility, to ufe and exercife martial*
" *difcipline*

" *difcipline and the law martial, in fuch cafes*
" *as occafion fhall neceffarily require and may*
" *legally be done, and to take and furprize,*
" *by all ways and means whatfoever, all and*
" *every fuch perfon or perfons, with their*
" *fhips, armour, ammunition, and other goods,*
" *as fhall in hoftile manner, invade or*
" *attempt the defeating or deftruction of the*
" *faid towns and places, or the hurt of any of*
" *our fubjects inhabiting there, or any of their*
" *fervants, or perfons employed by them, and,*
" *upon* JUST CAUSE, *to invade and deftroy*
" *enemies of the fame."*

Here feems to be granted as great a
latitude of pillage and deftruction as any
honeft man could wifh; and yet, in lefs
than five years, thofe gentlemen who had
the management of the Company's affairs
did not think it fufficient. This gave rife
to the Charter of the 31ft of his late
Majefty, commonly called *the Charter of
plunder;* of which, as it is the main pillar
of the extravagant pretenfions of the
majority of our prefent fet of Directors,

I fhall

I shall enter into a more particular discussion, and shall relate to you its history, as well as its contents.

When, upon the defeat and murder of Surajah Doula in 1757, much plunder was taken, some territory acquired, and a clear prospect opened to the Company, or, to speak more properly, to the Servants of the Company, of much more booty and much more territory, they began to be alarmed at their own good fortune; apprehending, and not without reason, that the British government would claim a share in those acquisitions. So, to secure to themselves whatever they might acquire, before the true value of it was known and attended to, the Directors thought it fit to apply by petition to his late Majesty.

The particular purposes of this petition were; first, to obtain an unlimited power of making war and peace with every Prince or people, not Christian, in the East Indies. To effect this, they thought
nothing

nothing could be more conducive than a precedent; fo they began their petition by fetting forth, "*That by feveral charters,* "*or letters patent, granted by his Majefty's* "*royal predeceffors to* FORMER *companies* "*trading to the Eaft Indies, fuch* FORMER "*companies have had power to fend fhips of* "*war to their fettlements in the Eaft Indies,* "*to raife and keep a military force, and to* "*make peace or war with any Princes or* "*people, not Chriftian, in any place of their* "*trade.*" This power of *making peace and war* had never, as is here confeffed, been granted to *this* company; fo, to find what is here alluded to, I was forced to fearch into the charters of *former* companies, and, at laft, found, in the charter of King CHARLES II. to a Company, very differently conftituted from the prefent, the following words: — "*To give power and* "*authority, by commiffion under their common* "*feal, or otherwife, to make peace or war* "*with any Prince or people, not Chriftians,* "*in any place of their trade, as fhall be moft*

C   "*for*

" *for the advantage and benefit of the said*
" *Governor and Company, and of their trade.*"
—A power dishonourable to the Company
that desired, to the lawyer who penned,
and to the King who granted it. Yet such
a power did our directors for the time
expect from King GEORGE the second
But they mistook their King, who was too
well acquainted with the laws of humanity
to empower a trading company to traffick
in the lives and fortunes of their fellow
creatures, upon so unjust and irrational a
distinction as that of their not having
embraced a revelation, which, to their
great misfortune, had never been revealed
to them. And, if they mistook the dispo-
sition of their King in supposing he might
consent to such a charter, they were no
less mistaken in supposing that men of
liberal minds, like Mr. PRATT and Mr.
YORKE, then Attorney and Solicitor
general, would ever lay such a charter
before him. And accordingly, although
the preamble to their Petition was adopted

as the preamble to the royal charter, the
unlimited powers alluded to in it were
never granted, or ever intended; as will
more fully appear in the course of these
observations.

As to the body of this petition it was
made up of two articles, one respecting
booty, the other respecting territory.

Concerning the booty, the words in
the petition run thus: " That your
" Majesty will be pleased to grant to the
" East India company, and their successors,
" all such plunder and booty as may be
" taken by any of their land or sea forces
" from any of your Majesty's enemies, or
" the Indian enemies of the said company,
" with the like exception as is contained
" in your Majesty's patent of the 17th
" September last." *   This clause was
admitted

* The patent here alluded to was given for the single
purpose of distributing certain booty, already taken in the
war carried on against the Nabob SURAJAH DOULA,
by the King's ships under Admiral Watson in conjunction
with the Company's troops under Colonel Clive.

admitted into the charter with three provifos, the reafons of which are fet forth by Mr. Pratt and Mr. Yorke in a letter they wrote to his Majefty, Dec. 24th 1757, accompanying the draught of the Charter.

The provisos are,

1. " Provided thofe captures are made " within the limits of the charter."

2. " Provided thofe captures are made " in a defenfive war, or during a ftate of " hoftility, commenced merely for the pro- " tection of their trade and fettlements. " *This is agreeable*, fay they, *to the terms* " *and intention of all the charters given to the* " *Company by your Majefty, or your royal* " *predeceffors, which empower them to make* " *war in the Eaft Indies, only to recompenfe* " *themfelves for loffes, or to repel invaders.*"
So that it is plain, from the opinions of thofe learned gentlemen who framed this charter, that the powers conveyed by it, of making peace and war, are not a jot more extenfive than thofe conveyed

to

to them by the former charters, the nature of which has been already explained.

3. " Provided that thofe captures are
" made by the Company's forces alone,
" and not in conjunction with thofe
" commiffioned by your Majefty's autho-
" rity; which will leave it in your Majefty's
" breaft, in cafe of joint expeditions, to
" diftribute the plunder or prizes made,
" amongft the officers, foldiers and fea-
" men in your fervice, and thofe employ-
" ed by the Company, according to their
" refpective merits, in fuch manner as
" may be agreeable to your royal wifdom."

Come we next to that part of the petition concerning territory, which runs
thus :   " That they may hold and enjoy,
" fubject to your Majefty's right of fove-
" reignty, all fuch fortreffes, diftricts
" and territories, as they have acquired,
" or may hereafter acquire, from any
" nation, ftate or people, by treaty, grant
" or conqueft; WITH power to reftore,
" give up, and difpofe of the fame, as they
                                   " fhall

" ſhall from time to time ſee occaſion;
" ſubject nevertheleſs to your Majeſty's
" diſpoſition and pleaſure as to ſuch lands
" as may be acquired by conqueſt from
" the ſubjects of any European power."

The firſt clauſe of this part of the petition, concerning the Company's obtaining
a right from his Majeſty, of holding the
territories they might acquire, was entirely rejected; and reaſons given for the
rejection by his Majeſty's learned ſervants,
in the following words: " In reſpect to
" ſuch territories as have been, or ſhall
" be acquired, by treaty or grant, from
" the great Mogul, or any of the Indian
" powers or governments, your Majeſty's
" letters patent are not neceſſary, the
" property of the ſoil veſting in the com-
" pany by the Indian grant, * ſubject only

" to

* The virtue here aſcribed, by the Attorney and Solicitor General, to grants from Indian Princes, can only be
meant of ſuch as have been procured from Princes who are
free from conſtraint, and who are poſſeſt both of the legal
and actual power of making their conceſſions good. But
of ſuch grants the Eaſt India company has never been
honoured

" to your Majesty's right of sovereignty,
" over the settlements, as English settle-
" ments, and over the inhabitants, as
" English subjects, who carry with them
" your Majesty's laws wherever they form
" colonies, and receive your Majesty's pro-
" tection by virtue of your royal charters.
" With respect to such places as have lately
" been acquired by conquest, the property,
" as well as the dominion, vests in your
" Majesty, by virtue of your known pre-
" rogative ; and, consequently, the Com-
" pany can only derive a right to them
" through your Majesty's grant. But we
" submit our humble opinion to your
" Majesty, that it is not warranted by
" precedent, nor agreeable to sound policy,
" nor to the tenor of the charters which
" have been laid before us, to make such
" a general grant not only of past, but of
" future

honoured with any, except that of the Emperor
FURRUKSEER in 1715, when he bestowed upon them
fifteen *begas*, or acres of land, wherever they should have
occasion to build factories.

" future contingent conquefts, made upon
" any power, European or Indian, to a
" trading company. Many objections
" occur to it, more material to be weighed
" than explained. If at any time the Eaft
" India company, in the profecution of
" their juft rights, fhall chance to conquer
" a fortrefs or diftrict which may be con-
" venient for carrying on their trade, and
" is afterwards either ceded to them by
" treaty, or proper to be maintained by
" force, it is time enough to refort to
" your Majefty, for your royal grant,
" whenever the cafe happens."

The latter claufe, concerning the power
of reftoring, giving up, and *difpofing of*
what they might conquer, was granted.
It had been afked, upon a doubt that the
Company was not enabled, by any of their
then fubfifting charters, to yield up conquefts made on the Indian Princes or
Governments, without his Majefty's li-
cence in every inftance, the procuring of
which might be attended with great
delay

delay in preffing exigencies : and it was granted, as appears from the letter juft cited, upon this humane principle, that although it might be dangerous to encourage the company to invade the lands of their neighbours, by allowing them to appropriate whatever they might fo lay hold on; yet to encourage them to make peace, could not be liable to objection; and the two learned gentlemen obferve, *that without this power of ceding what they had conquered, they might have the permiffion of making peace, without the means of obtaining it.* I cannot, however, avoid obferving, that this power, without a particular attention from His Majefty, is fubject to great abufe; efpecially in the hands of rapacious men, who, without caring for what is to follow, are defirous of returning to their own country with enormous fums of money acquired in a fhort time. The power of *difpofing* of what they conquer may eafily incline fuch men to conquer lands for the fake of *difpofing of them* to

D   the

the beft bidder; and I am not fure but
that the annals of India have already
furnifhed examples of fuch abufes *.

- And, indeed, without His Majefty's
particular attention to the conduct of the
Eaft-India Company abroad, not only
this, but all the former charters, might
ferve as authority for every degree of
cruelty and rapine. It is faid, for inftance, that the Company's officers may,
upon juft caufe, invade and deftroy their
enemies: but it could never be meant
that they fhould have the fole cognizance,
and be the fole judges of their own tranf-
greffions. Certainly not; for, if fo, the
fovereign power, exprefly referved by the
Charters, would virtually devolve upon
them: and they would be truly fovereign,
and anfwerable to God alone for the
injuftice of their wars; a pretenfion
which

---

* See Mr. Bolts's account of the ceffion of the Zemindary
of Bulwant Sing to Soujah al Doulah. *Confiderations
on Eaft-India affairs. Chap. iii. page 30.*

which I have not yet heard any Director bold enough to affert.

To return to my *Charter of Plunder*. It appears to me, upon a full confideration of it, with all its accompaniments, that the Directors were exceedingly unlucky in having obtained it ; for it certainly does not convey any Right of which they were not poffeffed before ; but, on the contrary, by their bringing forth this new charter, fo explained by thofe learned men, who had the framing of it, and fo underftood by the King when he gave it his Royal fanction, they have leffened the validity of King WILLIAM's charter, by which all their future acquifitions feem to have been fecured to them, as far as words can go, in the moft unlimited manner. For the charter of King WILLIAM fays, "*That* " *the Company fhall be a body politic and cor-* " *porate, capable in law to have, take, pur-* " *chafe, receive, hold, keep, poffefs, enjoy and* " *retain, to and for the ufe of them and their* " *fucceffors, any manors, meffuages, lands,* " *rents,*

" *rents, tenements, liberties, privileges, fran-*
" *chises, hereditaments and poſſeſſions whatſo-*
" *ever, and of what kind, nature and qua-*
" *lity ſoever ; and moreover to purchaſe and*
" *acquire all goods and chattels whatſoever,*
" *wherein they are not reſtrained by the ſaid*
" *act ; and alſo to ſell, grant, demiſe, alien*
" *or diſpoſe of the ſame manors, meſſuages,*
" *lands, rents, tenements, liberties, privileges,*
" *franchiſes, hereditaments, poſſeſſions, goods*
" *and chattels, or any of them.*" Here the
Company is authorized to *take, acquire and
retain, for their own uſe, all manner of lands,
rents or goods* ; and again, *to alien and diſpoſe
of,* at their pleaſure, all ſuch *lands, rents,
and goods* ; and this in ſuch a profuſion of
different terms, as if the whole words of
the language were to be guarantees for
this unlimited Right of acquiring and
alienating. It may be ſaid, indeed, and I
believe juſtly, that King William and
his learned council had it not in their
contemplation to permit, by any, or all of
thoſe words, that the Kingdoms of Bengal,

Bahar,

Bahar, and Oriſſa, ſhould be claimed as private property, or diſpoſed of as ſuch, by the Eaſt-India Company; or that the Crown ſhould not claim a Right of being conſulted in the diſpoſal of them or their revenues. But this reſervation would have equally ſubſiſted in whatever words the charter had been conceived, and would equally ſubſiſt under any new charter; the elementary principles in every government not only empowering, but requiring the ſupreme power to wave every conſideration of private Rights, whenever ſuch private Rights become, in a great degree, detrimental or dangerous to the public.

How far an Act of parliament might limit His Majeſty's known prerogative of making peace or war in any particular part of the globe, I will not take upon me to enquire. The enquiry is altogether foreign to the preſent ſubject, as no ſuch Act of parliament can be here alledged. The Right of appointing a *ſole* Plenipotentiary

tentiary for treating with Indian, as well
as with other Princes, is certainly still
vested in His Majesty; but the exercise
of such a Right would not fully answer
His Majesty's gracious purpose, which is
to assist the East-India Company, and to
assist them in such a way as their own
knowledge in their own affairs shall point
out to the judgment of his Servant, in
council and in concurrence with theirs.
Where there is a common interest of such
great importance, sound reason seems to
demand, that the care and deliberation
concerning it should be in common like-
wise : and it is to our reason His Majesty
is pleased to appeal, not in the tone of an
imperious master to his servants, but in
that of an indulgent parent to his
children.

You may perceive, my fellow Proprietors,
that in this long letter I have said very
little with regard to the expediency or
utility of the proposed measure. This is
owing

owing to my having obferved, that the controverfy, at our laft meeting, did not turn upon that point, but barely upon the impropriety of fuffering any encroachment to be made upon the Company's eftablifhed Rights. Were any encroachment intended upon the juft or legal Rights of the Company, there is no one would be feen more forward in their defence than myfelf, both as a friend to the Company, and as a friend to the ftate. The fecurity of private property, and of private rights of every kind, is the root of commerce, of population, of riches, and of ftrength in every ftate; and the ftatefman, who takes any ftep by which thofe private Rights are rendered precarious, difcovers himfelf to be but ill qualified for the place he fills. But here is no fuch invafion attempted; but, on the contrary, an attempt of private perfons to invade the Rights of the public, by challenging to themfelves a prerogative which belongs only to the heads of kingdoms and independent Republics. I have,

therefore,

therefore, endeavoured to shew you what
are in reality the Rights of the East-India
Company with regard to making peace
and war, by quoting what is to be found
in our several charters concerning them,
and shall now recapitulate and sum up the
whole, by observing :

That whatever passages are to be found in
those charters concerning peace and war,
are merely emanations of the royal Will and
Pleasure; no such being specified in the
Act of Parliament, which only authorizes
King William and his successors to grant
to the Company, from time to time, by
their letters patent, such powers and privileges as to him or them shall seem fitting.

That in none of those letters patent, or
charters, is it said, in express terms, that
the Company is absolutely empowered to
make war and peace; and that what is
mentioned in those charters concerning acts
of hostility, is strictly confined to such acts
of hostility as are for the defence of the
Company's property, retaliation of injuries,

or

or other *juft caufe,* the judgment of which cannot, in common fenfe, reft with the Company ; but falls to His Majefty, the fupreme Arbiter, by the Britifh conftitution, of all matters of peace and war.

That, although King WILLIAM and the fucceeding Kings of England, had not exprefly referved to themfelves their fovereign Right and Authority over the Eaft-Indian fettlements, and had granted to the Company the moft unlimited power of making war and peace; yet could they not, by any form of words, denude themfelves of that fovereign power, and could only be fuppofed to have delegated it to the Company, as to their Attorney or Plenipotentiary, till fuch time as it fhould be their royal pleafure to refume or limit it.

That, as by the Charters of the 13th of King GEORGE the firft, and of the 27th of King GEORGE the fecond, the Company is authorized *to invade and*

deftroy

deſtroy upon Juſt Cauſe only, and are particularly amenable to His Majeſty for any
breach of their Charter in this reſpect, it
is perfectly regular and neceſſary that His
Majeſty ſhould have complete knowledge,
from his own Officer, of the riſe and progreſs of all wars carried on in the Eaſt-
Indies, in order to know what wars are
carried on in compliance with the terms
of the Charter, and what not.

And laſtly, That when there is the
greateſt reaſon to believe, that the Company's Servants have made a greedy and
dangerous uſe of thoſe powers, we ought
to admire His Majeſty's goodneſs, who,
inſtead of depriving us of them altogether,
endeavours to interpoſe his fatherly care
in preventing any farther abuſe of them,

Before I conclude this paper, give me
leave, my fellow Proprietors, to add one
general Obſervation, which ſtruck me
on comparing together the ſeveral Charters
of the Eaſt-India Company, which is, that

in

in proportion as the *real* power of the Company increafed, its *legal* power and authority have been diminifhed. How far it will be for the advantage of the Proprietors, that Government fhould ftill proceed in narrowing the bounds of the Company's authority, I will not now enquire : but thofe who think farther limitations difadvantageous, will, in my humble opinion, find that the moft effectual method to prevent them, will be by ufing the power they ftill poffefs, with juftice and humanity towards thofe they call their fubjects in India ; and with mo-defty and obedience to thofe whom they ought to confider as their Rulers in Great Britain. I am, with great refpect,

Gentlemen,

Your moft obedient,

and moft humble Servant,

AN OLD PROPRIETOR.

London, Auguft 18,
1769.

www.ingramcontent.com/pod-product-compliance
Lightning Source LLC
Chambersburg PA
CBHW021453090426
42739CB00009B/1739

* 9 7 8 3 3 3 7 0 1 2 7 8 6 *